MW01518159

ONLINE PREDATORS

by Tammy Gagne

BrightP◆int Press

San Diego, CA

LIBRARY OF CONGRESS CATALOGING-IN-PUBLICATION DATA

Names: Gagne, Tammy, author.
Title: Online predators / by Tammy Gagne.
Description: San Diego, CA : BrightPoint Press, an imprint of ReferencePoint Press, Inc.,
    [2022] | Series: Protect yourself online | Includes bibliographical references and index. |
    Audience: Grades 7-9
Identifiers: LCCN 2021041480 (print) | LCCN 2021041481 (eBook) | ISBN 9781678202460
    (hardcover) | ISBN 9781678202477 (eBook)
Subjects: LCSH: Online sexual predators--Juvenile literature. | Internet--Safety measures--
    Juvenile literature. | Internet--Security measures--Juvenile literature.
Classification: LCC HV6773.15.O58 G34 2022 (print) | LCC HV6773.15.O58   (eBook) | DDC
    025.042028/9--dc23/eng/20211004
LC record available at https://lccn.loc.gov/2021041480
LC eBook record available at https://lccn.loc.gov/2021041481

CONTENTS

AT A GLANCE

- Online predators are people who use the internet to commit sexual crimes. They target children and teens.

- Even teens who are careful online can encounter a predator.

- Parents may forbid teens from talking to suspicious online friends. But that doesn't always end the relationships.

- Some online predators kidnap their victims. Then they sell them into sex trafficking.

- Predators are especially good at finding the most vulnerable young people.

- The most common behavior seen in online predators is grooming. This technique builds trust with the victim.

- A predator's ultimate goal is getting the victim to meet in person.

- Victims of online predators often start spending more and more time online. They may also become secretive about their online behavior.

- One way to avoid online predators is to keep one's social media accounts private.

- If a young person encounters an online predator, he or she should tell a trusted adult immediately.

JASMINE'S STORY

Jasmine was helping her mother put away groceries when her cell phone dinged. The familiar tone meant she had a new text message. When Jasmine picked up her phone, she saw a message from Aiden. He was a stranger she had accepted an online friend request from a week ago. Aiden said he was nineteen and in college.

Many teens are tempted to accept friend requests on social media even if they don't know the person in real life.

His social media profile photo showed him

sitting on a brand-new motorcycle. He

had promised to take her for a ride on it.

Jasmine had accepted the request because

If teens encounter an online predator, they should tell a parent or another trusted adult. They will be able to help.

Aiden was so cute. But something told her that meeting in person wasn't a good idea. She knew that some people on the internet weren't who they said they were.

When they first talked, Aiden asked Jasmine if she had a boyfriend. She admitted that she didn't. He said that she was beautiful. Aiden was smooth-talking. Part of her liked that. But it also scared her.

The text said he had a surprise for her. But before she could respond, her phone dinged again. A photo of Aiden without his clothes appeared on her screen. She didn't know what to do. If she told her mother she had accepted a friend request from a stranger, she might get in trouble. But she knew that the situation was getting out of hand. She decided just to tell her mother what was going on. This was clearly more than she could deal with alone.

DANGER LURKING ONLINE

The internet has made connecting with others very easy. People can text their friends any time of the day or night. Social media apps make it fun to chat and share photos and videos. Gamers enjoy playing online with friends. And people like watching others play games on Twitch.

It's fun to make new friends online. But not everyone online is a friend. Some people look for victims online. They seek to commit sexual crimes. They can create

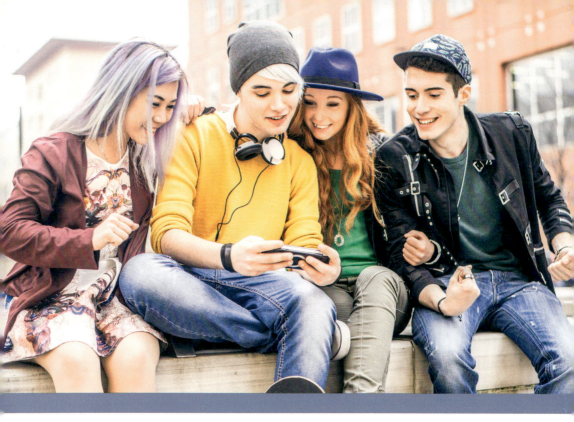

People can enjoy games and social media on the internet when they know how to avoid online predators.

dangerous situations for people of all ages. Children and teens are especially **vulnerable**. People should learn how to protect themselves against predators. It is possible to stay safe and enjoy connecting with others online.

CHAPTER ONE

WHO ARE ONLINE PREDATORS?

An online predator uses the internet to commit sexual crimes. Predators specifically target children or teens. Sometimes the crimes take place entirely online. Predators may share inappropriate photos of themselves. They may also ask young people to take and share

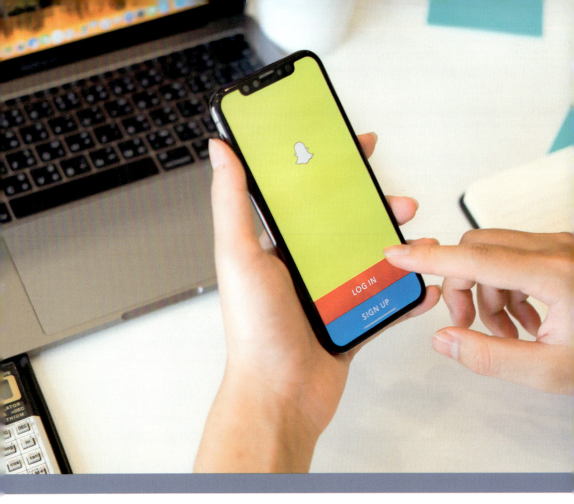

Online predators try to connect with potential victims through Snapchat and other social media apps.

inappropriate photos. Some predators ask

kids to meet up with them in person. A

number of dangerous things can happen

during a meeting. Predators may kidnap

their victims. They might force them into sexual activities or harm them in other ways.

SEARCHING FOR VICTIMS

The Child Crime Prevention & Safety Center studies online predators. It reports that about 500,000 predators are on the internet each day. They look for victims who share personal information online. Instagram, Snapchat, and TikTok are the most popular social media apps with teens. It only takes seconds for a predator to connect with a potential victim on these apps.

For example, a teen girl who plays soccer might post photos from her games.

A predator may create an account using

a fake name. He might use a profile photo

of a good-looking boy in a soccer uniform.

Then he might contact the girl through

ADDED RISK FROM THE PANDEMIC

The COVID-19 pandemic that began in 2020
created many challenges for kids. It placed
them at a greater risk for meeting online
predators. During the pandemic, schools were
closed to slow the spread of the disease.
Millions of students switched to online learning.
Their social interactions also shrank suddenly.
Kids couldn't see friends in person. They used
social media apps to stay in touch. These apps
became their primary gathering spots. All this
extra time online increased their chances of
dealing with online predators. Experts worried
that loneliness was driving some kids to take
more risks online.

REPORTS OF ONLINE PREDATORS: 2019 VS. 2020

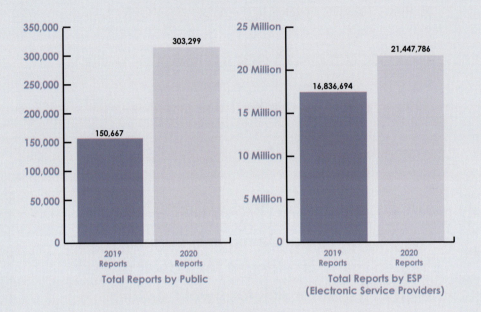

Total Reports by Public

- 2019 Reports: 150,667
- 2020 Reports: 303,299

Total Reports by ESP (Electronic Service Providers)

- 2019 Reports: 16,836,694
- 2020 Reports: 21,447,786

Source: National Center for Missing and Exploited Children, n.d. www.missingkids.org

During the pandemic, reports of online predators from the public and electronic service providers, such as Snapchat and TikTok, increased.

the app. The predator may talk about

soccer or compliment photos the girl has

posted. The girl might let her guard down.

She may begin sharing personal information with this stranger.

Even teens who are careful online can encounter predators. Lori Getz is a cyber education consultant. She explains, "Kids think that when they use social media, they're safe if they set it to private. But when they accept the requests of friends of friends, mutual friends . . . it's a different issue."[1]

THE KIDS MOST AT RISK

The most common targets of online predators are between twelve and fifteen years old. Many predators tell their victims

Predators give their victims lots of attention. They shower them with compliments and make them feel special.

that they are a few years older than that.

They do this because having a relationship

with someone older can appeal to teens.

It can make them feel cool and like an

independent adult. Predators often offer

excessive amounts of positive attention.

They make a point of flattering the victim.

"Teens want to be liked and belong. Positive

attention from someone can be really

compelling," says Christine Elgersma.[2] She

is a senior editor at Common Sense Media.

This organization teaches families how to

use technology safely.

Three-quarters of online predators'

victims are girls. But teen boys are at risk

too. In particular, those who are gay may

be targeted. These teens often find it

easier to talk about their sexuality online

than in real life. They might be afraid that

friends may not understand. If they fear being judged, reaching out blindly online may actually feel safer to them. But sharing personal information with strangers can be dangerous.

Predators choose their victims based on what they post online. They look for kids who share revealing photos or make suggestive comments. This implies that the kids are more open to talking about sex. Young people who post about past sexual abuse may also be targeted. Kids dealing with divorce are common victims too. Even teens who are just going through

Young people who are going through difficulties are at higher risk of being targeted. Predators give them emotional support to gain their trust.

a rough time with their parents may be

targeted. The predators see an opportunity.

They sense that kids are not getting

emotional support from their parents. So

they try to fill that void.

Kids can encounter predators almost anywhere online. Many predators look for victims on social media apps. Young people can also run into predators while gaming. Games designed for younger kids often have security settings. This prevents

PREDATORS LURK EVERYWHERE

Predators search for victims everywhere online. Kids without social media or gaming accounts can still be targeted. Police have even found online predators on homework help websites. These websites give students help with their schoolwork. Visitors are only supposed to discuss homework. But a predator will suggest continuing the discussion elsewhere. The predator may want to continue chatting on a messaging app. On those apps their conversations cannot be monitored.

players from contacting each other. But games aimed at older kids often allow players to chat freely. Kids curious about dating and sex might visit websites for adults. Predators look for young victims on these websites.

WHAT DOES AN ONLINE PREDATOR LOOK LIKE?

When people think of an online predator, they might imagine a creepy-looking, middle-aged man who lives alone. They may assume he has no job and spends nearly all his time on the internet. This is the stereotype of an online predator.

Most online predators are men. Nearly all of them work full-time. They look like ordinary people.

A *stereotype* is a widely held, simplified belief about a person. It is true that almost all online predators are male. But that is about the only thing that the stereotype gets right.

The National Juvenile Online Victimization Study analyzes online predators. The study's results are revealing. It shows that 91 percent of predators have full-time jobs. They go to work every day, just like most people do. Online predators also look like everyday people. Dr. Sarah Goode studies human society. She thinks that imagining that online predators look different makes people feel safer. She said, "We prefer to pretend it's 'those weird monsters over there.' And it hasn't helped us understand risks or keep children safe."[3]

The truth is that online predators can be attractive. They may also be smart, funny, and fun to talk to online. Predators are successful at luring young people into online communications because there is something appealing about them. Predators are often charming. They aim to make victims feel as though the predator is the only person who understands them. Predators use their charm and understanding to gain the trust of unsuspecting kids. They then use that trust to hurt them.

In some cases, the online predator isn't even a stranger. Many predators look for victims in their real lives. An online predator could be a sports coach or friend of a

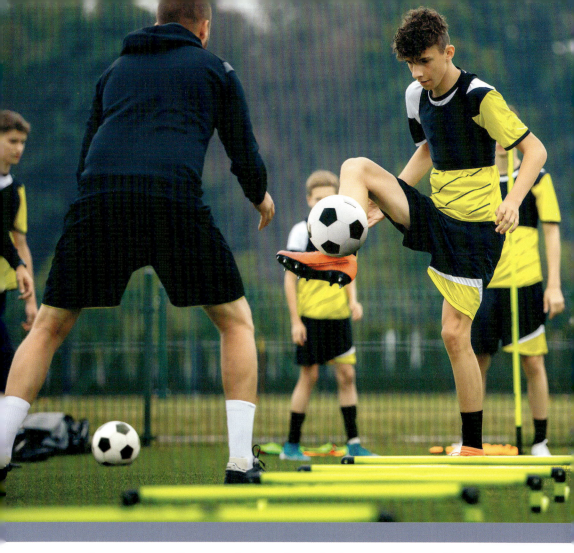

Sometimes the predator already knows the victim in real life. He could be a sports coach or another adult the victim has previously met.

friend. This type of predator might use his

real identity online. Or he may use a fake

name to enter the victim's online world.

CHAPTER TWO

WHAT IS THE HISTORY OF ONLINE PREDATORS?

The internet became a popular way to communicate in the late 1990s. Before this time, sexual predators had to seek out victims in person. This made approaching victims difficult because other people could see them. The internet made it possible

Once the internet became popular, teens began using it for gaming. However, online predators quickly began using the internet too.

for predators to hide. They could lurk in

chat rooms and other online spaces. All

anyone could see were their user IDs, which

they created themselves. It was simple for

predators to create fake identities. It is hard

for a forty-year-old man to pretend he is a

fourteen-year-old boy when everyone can

see him. But people can pretend to be

almost anyone online.

By the early 2000s, people were using the internet for gaming and socializing. One of the first popular social media platforms was MySpace. Millions of people flocked to this site. It allowed users to post photos and other details about their lives. Some users even posted their contact information. Later, Facebook launched and became even more popular. Police warned internet users to be careful using social media. They knew the internet was attracting predators as well.

AN ONLINE TRAGEDY

Alicia Kozakiewicz was thirteen years old when she left home in 2002. She left to meet a man she had met online. Her family had just gotten internet access. She saw it as a fun way to play online games with other people. Her parents had talked to her about the dangers strangers could pose. But strangers did not seem scary to her online. "People online may be strangers at first, but then you learn about them, and soon they seem like friends," she said.[4]

Alicia had been talking to this person for months. She thought he was a boy her age. But Scott Tyree was thirty-eight years old. He kidnapped Alicia and drove her to another state. There he hurt and

Like Alicia, many teens see the internet as a fun way to play games and meet new people online.

sexually assaulted her for four days. FBI

agents found her in the basement of

Tyree's townhouse. Tyree was arrested

and served seventeen years for the crime.

Alicia now works to educate people about

internet safety. She is an advocate for victims and missing persons.

BOYS CAN BE VICTIMS TOO

In 2013, Breck Bednar turned fourteen. He enjoyed playing computer games. He met up with friends online often. The only person in the group whom he didn't know in real life was Lewis Dayne. Dayne said he was seventeen. He claimed to be a computer engineer who owned a successful company. Breck's parents were suspicious of Dayne's story. But when they tried to end the online friendship, Breck resisted.

While girls are most often the target of online predators, boys can also be victims.

Over time, Breck stopped doing his chores and homework. He also talked about quitting school. Dayne said he could get Breck work at a software company. His mother asked the police to look into him.

Once online predators are convicted of crimes, they usually have to serve long prison sentences.

But they simply told her to make her son play a different online game. She tried to stop communication between Breck and Dayne. But Dayne secretly sent Breck a cell phone to make sure that wouldn't happen.

When Breck went to meet his online friend in person, Dayne murdered him. He then sent photos of Breck's body to two of the other boys in the gaming group.

Dayne was sentenced to twenty-five years in prison for the murder. Following his arrest, the Bednar family learned that he was actually eighteen. In 2011, Dayne had been accused of raping another boy. But charges were never filed in the incident.

Barry Bednar, Breck's father, was disappointed with the **authorities**. He said they wouldn't listen to him and Breck's mother. Barry also thinks that Breck's gender played a role. He said, "I believe that if Breck had been a girl, we'd have been taken more seriously."[5]

RAISING AWARENESS BY SHARING STORIES

In the early days of the internet, many people did not realize its power. They didn't understand the risks of going online. In 2010, actor and director David Schwimmer wanted to raise awareness about online predators. He made a movie about a girl who became a victim. *Trust* is based on the true story of Annie Cameron. At fourteen, she was raped by an adult man posing online as a sixteen-year-old boy.

The film shows how quickly a predator can form a relationship that feels real to a potential victim. Parents may forbid teens from talking to suspicious online friends. But that doesn't always end

SERVING TIME FOR THE CRIME

In 2014, Jordan James Kirby was arrested for crimes against girls. He met them online through fake social media accounts. His victims ranged from ten to fifteen years of age. He was convicted on six criminal counts against these victims. Kirby was sentenced to twenty-nine years in prison. The parents of one of the girls helped the FBI catch Kirby by reporting their suspicions.

the relationships. In many cases, a lot of these kids continue to secretly contact the predator, Schwimmer explained. The victim feels an emotional connection to the predator.

In 2013, another film also helped raise awareness about online predators. *Finding Faith* is a **fictionalized** story based on real-life situations. It's the story of a fourteen-year-old girl who strikes up an internet friendship. She thinks her new friend is a teenage boy. But the person is actually a predator. He kidnaps her with plans of selling her into **sex trafficking**.

Many victims feel as though they are in a real relationship with the predator. They don't realize that they are being manipulated.

Predators involved in sex trafficking search online for victims. They look for young people who are open to trusting strangers. Teens who have suffered abuse,

Predators often target vulnerable teens. They may try to involve them in sex trafficking.

have run away from home, or are already

dealing with other problems are often

vulnerable to predators. The predators

appear to care about the potential victims.

Predators work to build trust. Once victims

are kidnapped, the predators control them

with threats. They force victims to perform

sex acts. Many victims are even shipped

out of the country.

CHAPTER THREE

WHAT ARE THE WARNING SIGNS OF ONLINE PREDATORS?

P redators use a variety of ways to find their victims and start making a connection. Some predators search randomly on apps like Instagram and TikTok. They look for young people willing to talk to them online. They may pretend to be

Victims are often tricked into thinking they are chatting with someone their own age or just slightly older.

teens around the victim's age. Talking online

to other kids their own age seems safe to

most young people.

Predators may also pretend to be young

adults. A predator named Cort W. Davis

was in his early thirties when he met teen girls online. Davis told the girls that he was nineteen. In 2018, he sexually assaulted two girls. They were thirteen and fourteen years old. He was sentenced to twenty-five years in prison for the crimes.

LIES TOLD ONLINE

Some predators do not hide their true ages. But they do claim to be someone else. These predators may look for social media accounts that feature sports uniforms or carefully posed photos. Then they pretend to be athletic scouts or professional photographers looking for models.

Some online predators pretend to be professional photographers seeking young models. This convinces the teen to stay in contact.

The promise of fame and fortune can be

very tempting. It can convince victims to

keep talking to the predator.

Predators are especially good at finding

young people who are the most vulnerable.

Sarah Cooper was kidnapped by a human trafficker when she was in her midteens. She wasn't getting along with her parents well when she started talking to a predator on Facebook. She thinks he targeted her because she was going through a rough

ONLINE STALKING

Online predators do not target random victims. They look for young people whom they think will be the easiest to prey upon. Predators pay close attention to everything a young person says and does online. A predator may stalk a particular victim for weeks or even months. They will earn the victim's trust before asking to meet in person. They then use all the information they have gathered to start controlling the victim.

time. Now an adult, Sarah works with antitrafficking groups to warn young people about online predators. She says, "How predators win is because they survive in the dark. Once we shine a light on them, they can't win anymore. And you can take your power back."[6]

THE PATTERNS PREDATORS FOLLOW

Online predators often follow a pattern. It's useful to know about these warning signs. This can help young people avoid becoming a victim. It can also help family members or friends get help before someone they care about gets hurt.

The most common behavior seen in online predators is called **grooming**. This technique builds trust. In the beginning, predators do everything they can to make the victim feel comfortable and important. They give their victims large amounts of personal attention. This makes the victim feel like the predator cares. Predators also want their victims to think they have much in common. They may discuss movies, music, or other hobbies the victim enjoys.

In time, predators turn conversations toward sex. They do this to test the victim's boundaries. Many kids are naturally curious

The predator works to make the victim feel comfortable. The predator pretends to have lots in common with the victim.

about sexuality. Predators take advantage

of this. They may send sexually **explicit**

photos or videos or ask the victim to take

photos and share them.

As the relationship develops, the predators may ask the victim for pictures.

Soon predators begin driving wedges between the victims and their family and friends. A predator may tell victims their parents don't understand them. The predator might suggest that the victims' friends don't like them as much he does.

Predators want to alienate their victims from others. They don't want anyone to interfere with their ultimate goal. That goal is meeting victims in person.

FBI agent Peter Brust told PBS that 83 percent of victims meet their predators willingly. But he pointed out that predators work hard to manipulate these teens. He said it's unfair to expect teens to match wits with a much older adult. Brust believes the victims are brainwashed.

COMMON BEHAVIOR OF VICTIMS

Family and friends may notice changes in the victim's behavior. This too follows a pattern. It begins with spending more and more time online. When parents try to limit internet usage, a victim might become upset. Some victims will even lash out with an angry outburst. The victim may act secretively when using the computer. Whenever a family member walks by, the victim may close the web browser or shut the laptop.

Victims may start withdrawing from their real-life relationships. They stop having time for friends or family. Instead, they always seem to be online or texting. Victims may make phone calls to numbers parents don't

Some victims may be so wrapped up in the relationship with the predator that they spend all their time online.

recognize. They might receive calls from a

friend the parents don't know. They may

also receive gifts from the predator.

At first, the victim may worry that parents

will find out about the relationship. At this

stage, the victim might still believe the

predator is a friend. But this changes when

the victim doesn't do what the predator

wants. Predators start manipulating victims

more directly. Many use sexual extortion,

also known as sextortion. Victims have

often already sent photos of themselves

to the predator. Now the predator may

threaten to show the photos to the victim's

parents unless the victim agrees to send

NOT THE VICTIM'S FAULT

It is common for the victims of online predators to feel like the situation is their fault. They may blame themselves for keeping the online relationship a secret or for not seeking help soon enough. But it is never the victim's fault. The only person to blame is the predator.

Victims may feel trapped and that they are forced to do what the predator is demanding of them.

more pictures or meet in person. Some

predators even threaten to hurt people the

victim cares about. When this happens,

the victim may feel forced to continue the

relationship with the predator. The victim

feels trapped and fears the predator will follow through with these threats.

It is important for the victim to seek help. It is dangerous to meet a stranger in person. In addition, sextortion poses serious risks to the victim's mental health. Many victims feel overwhelmed. They see no way out of the situation. They may even try to take their own lives.

Anyone who suspects that they or a loved one may be dealing with an online predator should end all communication immediately. It is also important to report the situation to the police. Common Sense

The victim needs to reach out for help. A trusted adult can help the victim deal with the situation and file a police report.

Media's Christine Elgersma wrote about the topic. She said that victims should always file a police report. This is even if the victims don't want to make a big deal out of it. Reporting the predator helps to keep him from harming others.

CHAPTER FOUR

HOW CAN I PROTECT MYSELF FROM ONLINE PREDATORS?

A s long as the internet exists, online predators will continue to use it to find victims. But internet users can do things to protect themselves. One of the most important is keeping all online accounts private. This includes social

People should be careful to keep their online accounts private. This helps to protect them from online predators.

media and gaming accounts. Predators do

their homework. They study social media

profiles to learn about their potential victims.

They look for young people who have

suggestive profile photos. Predators also

seek out young people who share personal

information online.

FALSE FRIENDS

Some predators will send friend requests to

people they don't know. They often create

a false identity to do this. The first goal is

just getting the potential victim to accept the

AGAINST THE LAW

A predator may have broken the law even without meeting a victim in person. While ages differ by state, minors are protected by law. It is illegal to send sexually explicit material to minors. It is also illegal to distribute child pornography. This includes photos or videos of a minor without clothes or doing a sexual act.

friend request. Then the predator can gain access to the potential victim's photos and other posts.

Sometimes internet users meet strangers in public forums. These can be chat rooms, bulletin boards, or community pages. While visiting these online spaces, users should be cautious. They should never post any identifying personal information. It is very important not to share addresses or phone numbers. Even sharing the name of one's school or sports team can be risky. Online predators can use this type of information to locate young people in person that they have seen online.

When young people want to talk about something personal, they should stay away from the internet. Instead, they should talk to a family member or real-life friend. This is even if the young person thinks the online friend can be trusted. It's always safer to speak to someone in real life.

ENCOUNTERING A PREDATOR

Some young people visit chat rooms or dating apps meant for adults. They may be curious about romantic relationships or sex. Some teens even dare friends to

It's always best for people to discuss private topics in person with family or friends.

start conversations with strangers online.

They think this is a fun and harmless

game. It may feel exciting to visit adult

websites. And it may seem fun to strike

up conversations with strangers. But this

behavior can put young people in contact

with sexual predators.

If young people are approached by online predators, they need to end all communication immediately. Then they should tell an adult. This is a smart move, even if they think the problem has been

CYBERTIPLINE

The National Center for Missing and Exploited Children offers help for victims. It runs a tip line for young people who have been contacted by online predators. They can report a predator by calling 1-800-THE-LOST. Victims can also visit the center's website at www.missingkids.org. The center can put victims in touch with others who have dealt with predators. Many young people who have been victimized by an online predator feel alone. They don't think anyone can understand them. Talking to others who have been in the same situation can help.

If young people have been contacted by an online predator, they should tell an adult immediately.

solved. A parent, a teacher, or even an older

sibling can help. They can make sure the

young person is safe from harm.

A young person who has willingly entered

a relationship with an online predator may

be scared. They may think it's too late to

ask for help. Victims may feel embarrassed. They may worry that they have done something wrong. They may think their parents will be mad if they find out. But it is never too late to tell someone about a predator's actions.

WHERE TO SEEK HELP

Once the young person has told a trusted adult, the next step is reporting the predator. People should start with local police. These officers can document the situation. They will try to locate the predator. Because predators often use **aliases** online, this step can take some time. But it

Help is available for young people dealing with online predators. If they don't have a trusted adult to talk with, they should call 1-800-THE-LOST.

doesn't mean the police won't be able to track the predator down.

Police have procedures for the next steps that should be taken. These may include reporting the incident to the internet platform where the communication took place. Many websites and apps allow people to block users they have had trouble with. This too is a smart step. But timing is crucial. When a report is filed, the platform will likely shut down the predator's account. This can cause the predator to erase evidence. They may start using a different name online. These actions can make it harder for the police to catch the predator.

In 2019, a girl named Ella from New York was approached by an online predator on Instagram. He sent her explicit photos of himself. Then he demanded that she do the same. Ella told her mother, who contacted Instagram about the incident. The company

After reporting the online predator to the police, the victim can also file a report with the internet platform.

quickly removed the predator's account.

But this move created problems for the

police. New York Detective Andrew Shore

says, "It was really frustrating when we

found out the account was deleted. We

knew so much crucial evidence was

wiped."[7] The police were unable to catch this predator.

It is also wise to save all emails or screenshots of other communication with the predator. The police may be able to use this information to track down the predator. If charges are filed, this proof could also become important legal evidence.

Online predators will always lurk on the internet. But knowing how they operate can help young people avoid them. Knowing what to do when contacted by a predator isn't just helpful. It could literally save a young person's life.

Victims should report an online predator to the police. The police will work to catch the predator so he doesn't harm other people.

GLOSSARY

aliases

false names used by a criminal

authorities

people in command; police

convictions

formal rulings that find a person guilty of a crime

explicit

showing nudity or sexuality

fictionalized

made into fiction

grooming

performing actions that help a predator gain a victim's trust

sex trafficking

the illegal business of recruiting and transporting a person for the purpose of sex

vulnerable

capable of being physically or emotionally wounded

SOURCE NOTES

CHAPTER ONE: WHO ARE ONLINE PREDATORS?

1. Quoted in Nicole Fabian-Weber, "8 Dangers of Social Media to Discuss with Kids and Teens," *Care*, March 2, 2021. www.care.com.

2. Quoted in Christine Elgersma, "How to Talk to Teens About Dealing with Online Predators," *Common Sense Media*, August 25, 2020. www.commonsensemedia.org.

3. Quoted in Adam Forrest, "Why Do We Assume Pedophiles Look a Certain Way?," *Vice*, February 4, 2015. www.vice.com.

CHAPTER TWO: WHAT IS THE HISTORY OF ONLINE PREDATORS?

4. Quoted in Alicia Kozakiewicz, "Kidnapped by a Paedophile I Met Online," *BBC*, March 6, 2016. www.bbc.com.

5. Quoted in Anna Moore, "I Couldn't Save My Child From Being Killed by an Online Predator," *The Guardian*, January 23, 2016. www.theguardian.com.

CHAPTER THREE: WHAT ARE THE WARNING SIGNS OF ONLINE PREDATORS?

6. Quoted in Cheryl Wills, "Trafficking Survivor Shares Story About How Predators Groomed Her on Social Media," *Spectrum News NY1*, June 17, 2021. www.ny1.com.

CHAPTER FOUR: HOW CAN I PROTECT MYSELF FROM ONLINE PREDATORS?

7. Quoted in Melissa Russo, "I-Team: When Predators Target Children Online, Feds Urge Parents to Report It to Them First," *NBC New York*, January 31, 2019. www.nbcnewyork.com.

FOR FURTHER RESEARCH

BOOKS

Carrie Anton, *Smart Girl's Guide: Digital World: How to Connect, Share, Play, and Keep Yourself Safe*. Middleton, WI: American Girl Publishing, 2017.

Ashley Nicole, *Privacy and Social Media*. Broomall, PA: Mason Crest Publishing, 2019.

Janine Ungvarsky, *The Risks of Social Media*. San Diego, CA: BrightPoint Press, 2022.

INTERNET SOURCES

"6 Things Every Teen Needs to Know About Sexting," *Verywell Mind*, December 10, 2020. www.verywellmind.com.

"Online Predators: What Do We Know, and What Can We Do?," *National Center for Health Research*, n.d. www.center4research.org.

"Teens and Sexting: Know the Facts," *Nationwide Children's Hospital*, n.d. www.nationwidechildrens.org.

WEBSITES

Crimes Against Children Research Center
www.unh.edu/ccrc

This organization combats crimes against children by providing research and statistics to policy makers, law enforcement agencies, child welfare advocates, and the public. This data includes information about abduction, homicide, assault, and physical and sexual abuse.

Federal Bureau of Investigation
Crimes Against Children/Online Predators
www.fbi.gov/investigate/violent-crime/cac

The FBI plays an active role in investigating child abductions and counteracting the sexual exploitation of children.

National Center for Missing & Exploited Children
www.missingkids.org

This nonprofit organization works to find missing children, reduce sexual exploitation, and prevent child victimization. It provides assistance and support for victims and their families.

INDEX

IMAGE CREDITS

ABOUT THE AUTHOR

Tammy Gagne has written dozens of books for both adults and children. She lives in northern New England with her husband, her son, and a menagerie of pets.